Never again be afraid to Dream
Never again be afraid to Plan

The
Five Minute
Business
Plan©

CAROLE SALLID-TIMES, MHS

The Five-Minute Business Plan

Copyright © 2005 by Carole Times, MHS

Dream to be Seen poem Courtesy of Jerald Times, www.dabadmansongs.com

This book is dedicated to the Professors at

Lincoln University's Grad School

Who did not teach me *what* to think,

They taught me *how* to think.

Thank you, Lincoln U

THE FIVE-MINUTE BUSINESS PLAN©

TABLE OF CONTENTS

If the dream affords the dreamer some light on himself,

It is not the person with closed eyes

who makes the discovery

but the person with open eyes

to fit thoughts together

Michael

Leiris

Making plans is something we do all the time. We plan our day, we plan our meals, we plan our work on the job and even plan our night out with the guys and girls. Yet when it comes to creating a plan for our business, we push it aside, literally and figuratively, hoping we can deal with it at a more propitious time. Did you tell yourself that planning is just not what you do or, for that matter, ever want to do? Then this work/study book was created with you in mind.

Think about this, you wouldn't dare build a house without a plan How then can you build a business without a written thought as to what it will cost, what are the future goals of your business or what impact it will have on your life and the world. Even if you decided that writing a plan is not your forte and giving it to a professional is a much better idea, that professional writer would do a much finer job if you put the salient points of your prospective business on paper. I have found that the only thing worse than not creating a plan and letting your dream die, is opening and operating a business without a plan and letting the business die.

The following *Five Minute Business Plan* work/study book is the answer to your putting off getting started. It is not meant to replace the 30 plus pages of a regular business plan. It is intended to give you a quick way to jump-start your thoughts, cast aside your fear of planning, and to evaluate the soundness of your ideas. This work/study book gives you many questions you have to answer yourself. It encourages you to be creative and explore the answers. Think of it as homework.

This book presupposes that you, the entrepreneur, have already decided that you are ready, willing and able to start a business and that you have already passed the place where you are just toying with your business idea. While qualities/skills such as being well organized are good to have when you're starting a business and to run a successful business, they are not rated that highly by successful entrepreneurs. When asked which traits contributed most to success, being willing to take the initiative ranked highest.

Surprisingly, a strong desire for money actually ranked near the bottom of the list.

Many times this workbook will ask you to visualize your idea. This step is too important to overlook. The clearer the picture you have and the more often you see it in your mind, the more your creative subconscious will work for you to achieve your goals. Try it now. Visualize in your mind and then on paper how your store or office will appear in reality; visualize your product and how people will appreciate it; visualize your mailbox full of orders, customers constantly calling. The first Law of Attraction is visualization. Why? Because it works!

By the way, *The Five Minute Business Plan* can be used to plan almost anything: a birthday party, a church fundraiser or your company's next sales strategy. This workbook, however, will focus on the entrepreneurial business plan.

Again, *The Five-Minute Business Plan* is not meant to replace the standard business plan. It is meant to teach you how to quickly process your idea, your dream, and determine the soundness of your vision. After you have mastered the basics of *The Five-Minute Business Plan,* all it takes is five minutes in your head or on paper to start planning any business idea, decide if the business idea is worthy of follow-up and, if so, confidently take the next steps to enhance this basic plan. Or you can use this basic plan to develop a standardized business plan or have someone else create your full-size business plan with clear paradigms.

Carole Sallid Times, MHS

STEP I: PURPOSE

If you can imagine it, you can create it. If you can dream it, you can become it."

William Arthur Ward

- ## The Mission Statement

Someone says, "Wow, wouldn't this be a good thing for mankind? And guess what?" they said, "I could even make money doing this!" And a business idea is started. Your mission statement tells the world your company's reason for being, your purpose, your dream. To succeed, your mission should also be your passion, something you would follow to the end, no matter what.

The mission statement can be a few sentences or a few paragraphs in length. It should include: your company's purpose, description of how you intend to carry out the purpose, why you do it and the desired result.

The important thing is that you state your ideas clearly to the world. Your mission statement should be uplifting, motivating you and those in your company to realize and live your company's dream. This mission statement is also important because it helps the financiers understand your mind-set. The mission statement of your business helps form your vision statement.

Examples of Mission Statements

"McDonald's vision is to be the world's best quick service restaurant experience. Being the best means providing outstanding quality, service, cleanliness, and value, so that we make every customer in every restaurant smile. *McDonald's*

Our goal is to be a retailer with the ability to see opportunity on the horizon and have a clear path for capitalizing on it. To do so, we are moving faster than ever before, employing more technology and concentrating on those elements most important to our core customers." *Macy's Department Store*

WRITE YOUR
MISSION STATEMENT HERE

Tip: A Mission Statement should be short, clear, vivid, inspiring and concise

- ## The Vision Statement

The vision statement can also be called a Value Statement. When you create a vision statement you are articulating your future dreams, hopes and values for your business. The vision should capture your dream and take it soaring. It reminds you, and tells the world, what you are trying to build. It can also serve as a roadmap for strategic company planning. A vision statement could be for a one-year, two-year or five-year period. It could be a vision for infinity. It could be for the entire company or a division of the company.

The vision statement is not for outsiders; it is mainly for you and the members or your company. In a not-for-profit your organization's vision is for the future you want to create for the *community* you wish to impact.

Example of a Vision Statement

To achieve sustainable growth, we have established a vision with clear goals.

Profit: Maximizing return to shareowners while being mindful of our overall responsibilities.

People: Being a great place to work where people are inspired to be the best they can be.

Portfolio: Bringing to the world a portfolio of beverage brands that anticipate and satisfy peoples; desires and needs.

Partners: Nurturing a winning network of partners and building mutual loyalty.

Planet: Being a responsible global citizen that makes a difference.

GM's vision is to be the world leader in transportation products and related services. We will earn our customers' enthusiasm through continuous improvement driven by the integrity, teamwork, and innovation of GM people.

General Motors

WRITE YOUR VISION STATEMENT HERE

Tip: Your statement needs to be positive and inspirational. Learning how to write a Vision Statement takes time! It might be tedious but is an important task.

Other factors to consider

Will your business be:
- A corporation (S Corp, C Corp, or LLC)
- DBA (Dong Business As) –Business Certificate
- Sole Proprietor/Partnership

STEP II: PRODUCT/SERVICE

"Keep spiritually sound and be persistent.
Persistence is the key.
Just never stop believing in your dream."
Deborah Aquila

Your product or service is the realization of your vision. It is your dream in action. You must ask yourself some tough questions about your services and/or products such as:

- What services or products will I sell?
- Is it in demand? If not,
- Can I create a demand for my service/product
- What skills, experience do I bring to the business?
- Will I be able to deliver it better than anyone else?

NAME YOUR BUSINESS:

_____

(When you are set on a business name, do a preliminary check with the Secretary of State's office in your state to see if the name is available. This can be done on the Internet.)

BRIEFLY DESCRIBE THE PRODUCT(S) SERVICE(S) YOUR BUSINESS WILL SELL

_____

_____

_____

_____

DRAW A PICTURE OF YOUR FINISHED PRODUCT(S) OR, IF POSSIBLE, YOUR SERVICE(S)

Tip: If you think you cannot draw, take a picture (closest you can get to your product) from a magazine, the Internet or a newspaper.

Competitive Advantage:

Competitive Advantage, the pundits say, is an advantage that a firm has over its competitors, allowing it to generate greater sales or margins and/or retain more customers than its competition. In other words, what makes your product or service different than the other guy? Why will people come to your company to purchase your product or service?

There can be many types of competitive advantages including the firm's cost structure, product offerings, distribution network and customer support.

Strongly consider why your product/service is unique. It could mean the difference between success or failure; big profits or just getting by.

What is your Product's or Service's Competitive advantage?

PRODUCT/SERVICE   **COMPETITIVE ADVANTAGE**

_____   _____

_____   _____

_____   _____

_____   _____

_____   _____

STEP III – PLACE

"If you have built castles in the air, your work need not be lost; that is where they should be.
Now put foundations under them."
Henry David Thoreau

Various factors need to be considered when choosing an office space. If you are selling product from a store then the most likely place for your office would be the store's location. However, home businesses are very popular now and if you do not need space for inventory or you do have enough space in your home to store your product, or you are just selling product or service from a website, then a home office has its advantages.

However, the first thought when starting a business should be Location! Location! Location! Almost nothing is important in your plan as where you will sell your service or product or where you have your office. Before you start your business you should do a market analysis (see below). The tough questions to ask are:

- Who are my customers? Where are they located?
- Where will my business/office be located? Do customers have to come to my office?
- From what location(s) will I sell my product/service?
- Where is my competition located?
- Will my business have access to transportation, pedestrian traffic, or parking? Is it safe? Appropriate zoning?
- Do I need an office? Can I work at home?
- Can the website/computer be my only store/office?
- Do I need permits/Licenses to sell?

MARKET ANALYSIS

"Failing to plan is planning to fail"
Alan Lakein

Customers:

What is the age range of your target
customer?_____

What is the gender of your target
customer?_____

What is the income level of your target
customer?_____

Where does your target customer
live/work?_____

Who does your target customer buy from
now?_____

Competition

Who are your competitors?

_____

How are their prices compared to yours?

_____

How is their customer service compared to yours?

_____

What do your potential customers think of them?

_____

What is their greatest strength?

_____

What will your business specifically do to beat the competition?

_____

DESCRIBE YOUR OFFICE LOCATION AND WHY YOU CHOSE THIS SITE

Office Location(s)

_____

_____

_____

_____

DRAW A PICTURE OF YOUR OFFICE, HOME OFFICE (INSIDE OR OUT)

Check all the ways that you plan on selling in your business

FROM A STORE   _____
          TELEPHONE SALES   _____

FLEA MARKETS   _____
          BY APPOINTMENT   _____

ONE ON ONE   _____
          THROUGH A CATALOG   _____

DOOR-TO-DOOR   _____
          FROM YOUR HOME   _____

DIRECT MAIL   _____
          TV ADS   _____

COLD CALLS   _____
          INTERNET   _____

RADIO AD   _____
          INTERNAL SALES TEAM   _____

SCHOOL FAIR   _____
          HEALTH FAIR   _____

IN ANOTHER STORE   _____
          OTHER   _____

How will your store look? Draw the outside/inside of your store.

STEP IV – PRICE

If money is your hope for independence you will never have it.
The only real security that a man will have in this world is a
reserve of knowledge, experience, and ability.
~Henry Ford

<u>Start Up Costs</u>

The financial part of your business plan allows you to estimate the amount of money you need to get started and the approximate amount you need for the maintenance of the business. A good financial plan helps raise money and helps the business to run in the black. Lack of financial planning can destroy a business.

The last thing you want to do is underestimate the amount of money you need to start your business. You'd never get off the ground. When you are ready to do a standard business plan, you should consult an accountant if you do not feel comfortable with numbers.

If your business is a partnership, your agreement should contain the amount of funds each partner is putting up and how much money should be borrowed, if needed.

If your business is a corporation, I strongly suggest you contact an accountant to determine if and how much of borrowed funds will be financed by stock or debt.

If you are a sole proprietor you should state that in your general overview of your standard business plan.

As you can see, the basis for funding the business depends on the legal structure of your business, the amount to be raised and whether the business is funded by a loan or by its owners/investors. Below is a quick worksheet for initial start-up cash requirements. Rely on your planning so far to estimate the amounts needed.

Start-up Dollars Needed

Advertising .... $_____
    (Promotion for opening business)

Beginning Inventory ....   _____
    (Inventory needed to open)

Cash ....   _____
    (Cash you need for the register)

Decorating..............................   _____

Deposits................................   _____
    (Utilities, lease, telephone, etc)

Fixtures/Equipment ....   _____

Installation Costs.......................   _____

Insurance................................   _____

Lease Payments
    (Amount to be paid before opening)...   _____

Licenses & Permits........................   _____
    (Check with state and local offices)

Professional Fees.........................   _____
    (Lawyer, CPA, etc)

Services..................................   _____
    (Cleaning, accounting, etc)

Supplies..................................   _____
    (Office, cleaning, etc.)

Unanticipated expenses   _____

TOTAL $ ========

FIXED COSTS PER MONTH

You will also need money to keep you in business for at least three months (some would say six months –your choice here) or until you start turning a profit. Consider these fixed costs of your business and times them by 3 or 6.

Advertising   _____

Bank fees/Credit Card fees   _____

Delivery charges   _____

Insurance/Legal   _____

Inventory   _____

Loan Payments/Interest   _____

Office Expense   _____

Rent /Mortgage Payments   _____

Salaries - Staff   _____

Salaries – Owner, Manager   _____

Supplies   _____

Telephone/Utilities   _____

Unanticipated expenses   _____

Other_____   _____

           Total Monthly fixed Costs $_____

Total Fixed Costs x 3 months = $_____*

Total Fixed Costs x 6 months = $_____

* The amount of Initial Capital needed to start your business is a total of Start Up Costs and Three to Six Months (you choose how many months) of Fixed Costs.

GETTING MONEY

Funding Your Business

You need money to make money. This is invariably where the dream is lost. Most of us give up when we can't find the money to capitalize our business. If you personally lack the capital to fund your business, there are many other ways to obtain it :

- government loans (SBA),
- grants ,
- corporations,
- investors
- bank loans,
- family, friends,
- credit unions,
- venture capitalists,
- your 401K,
- partners

Be persistent, knock on any door! Look everywhere! Most new businesses ideas fail not only because of the lack of sufficient capital but the lack of persistence as well.

It is often said that small business people have a difficult time borrowing money. This is true. Banks make money by lending money. However, the inexperience of small business owners in financial matters often prompts many banks to deny loan requests. To be successful in obtaining a loan, you must be prepared and organized. You must know exactly how much money you need, why you need it and how you can pay it back. You must be able to convince your lender that you are a good credit risk. Requesting a loan when you are not properly prepared sends a signal to your lender. That message is ... "High Risk!" Take time with the financial part of your business plan. If you are not good with numbers, hire someone who is.

MAKING MONEY

Everyone knows profit is a good thing. It's what our economy is founded on. Profit is simply making more money than you spend to sell or manufacture your product or service. But of course nothing's ever really simple, is it?

It might seem like a no-brainer to define just exactly what profit and loss are. But of course these have definitions like everything else. Profit can be called different things, for instance it's sometimes called net income or net earnings. Businesses that sell products and services generate profit from the sales of those products or services and from controlling the attendant costs of running the business. Showing a profit, or a positive figure on your balance sheet is of course the aim of every business. It's what our economy and society are built on.

It doesn't always work out that way. Shifts in assets and liabilities are important to owners and executives of a business because it's their responsibility to manage and control such changes. Making a profit in a business involves several variables, not just increasing the amount of cash that flows through a company, but management of other assets as well.

Profit is also sometimes called taxable income. It is the job of the accounting and finance professionals to assess the profits and losses of a company. They have to know what created both and what the results of both sides of the business equation are. Evaluate the success of your business based on profit, not revenue. It doesn't matter how many thousands of dollars you are bringing in each month if your expenses are almost as high, or higher. Many high-revenue businesses have gone under for this very reason -- don't be one of them.

Pricing

Pricing your product or service is probably one of the trickiest parts of your business. This weighs heavily on your profit and loss. You must be careful not to overprice or price below or under the competition. There are several known strategies such as price lining or multiple pricing you can follow. Ask your accountant or research them through the Internet or the library.

Retail Cost and Pricing: Follow the manufacturer's suggested retail price. This method does not account for the element of competition.

Pricing Below Competition: This strategy reduces the profit margin per sale. It also requires that you reduce your cost. Exposes you to price wars you might not win.

Pricing Above Competition: Use this when the customer's greatest concern is not price. Other customer considerations might be speed of delivery or service, friendly employees, knowledge of product or service.

Price Lining: This strategy targets a precise segment of the buying public by carrying products in a specific price range only. For example, a store may wish to attract customers willing to pay more than $100 for a pair of shoes.

Multiple Pricing: This approach involves selling a number of units for a single price, like the $99 cents stores or two items for $1.98. This could be used for sales and year-end clearances and should be used on low cost consumer products like toothpaste or shampoo.

Pricing Your Service: The primary difference between offering products and services is that, in many instances, potential customers may be able to perform the service themselves (i.e. moving, real estate, painting, cleaning). You must, therefore, provide your service in a faster, more convenient, and less expensive manner than your competition or even your customer could. In addition to pricing for your target market, you should also take into account seasonality.

Tip:
Remember the old saying:
> You want to offer products/services that don't come back and to offer them to people who do.

OPERATIONS

You should operate your business like a business. Tough questions for you to answer:

- What will be your legal structure? __single owner ___ partnership ___corporation (what kind)_____

- How will my company's records be maintained?
_____

- What equipment and supplies will I need?
_____

- Where will the product be made/who will perform the service? _____

- How is the product/service delivered?_____
_____

- Who will administer the business/how will it operate on a day-to-day basis?

_____

- How will I compensate myself?
_____

- Who will be the key people in my business?

_____

STEP V - PROMOTION

Keep sowing your seed,
For you never know which will grow-
Perhaps it all will
Ecclesiastes

How will you promote your business? How do you intend to make it grow? After you have identified what makes your business different than others, organize promotional activities and develop short and long term sales goals.

Check all the ways you plan on advertising your business.

Business Cards   _____
     Internet   _____
     (Email blasts)

Internet Search Engines _____
     (i.e. Google, Yahoo, etc.)

Word of Mouth   _____
     Magazine ads   _____

Flyers   _____
     TV/Cable ads   _____

Posters   _____
     Newspaper ads   _____

Billboards   _____
     Yellow pages   _____

Radio Ads   _____
     School paper   _____

Promotional give-aways   _____
     Bulletin Boards   _____
     (T-shirts, key chains or pens, etc.)
     (Supermarkets, churches, etc.)   _____

Social Networking Sites _____
        (i.e. Facebook, You Tube, Twitter, Linked In, etc.)

Internet Search Engines _____
        (i.e. Google, Yahoo, etc.)
        Other   _____

A Note on Networking:

While networking can be done in a number of ways, teleconference, Internet Webinars, Chat rooms, blogs, etc., (and these should not be overlooked) one of the best ways is person to person. By meeting people face to face you can give out your brochure, flyers, business cards and talk to people about your business. List organizations you could join to help you meet people and network.

Organization	Do They Have Meetings?	Tel #/Contact
_____	(Y) (No)	_____
_____	(Y) (No)	_____
_____	(Y) (No)	_____
_____	(Y) (No)	_____

**DRAW A SAMPLE BUSINESS CARD
FOR YOUR COMPANY
Make sure to include your Logo?**

DRAW A SAMPLE FLYER OR BROCHURE FOR YOUR BUSINESS

CREATE A CLASSIFED AD FOR YOUR SERVICE OR PRODUCT
(No more than 25 words)

WRITE A PRESS RELEASE FOR YOUR PRODUCT OR SERVICE

Tip: Be sure to communicate the 5 Ws and the H. Who, what, when, where, why, and how. Then consider the points below if pertinent.

Sample Press Release:

FOR IMMEDIATE RELEASE:
Contact:
Contact Person
Company Name
Telephone Number
Fax Number
Email Address
Web site address

Headline

City, State, Date — Opening Paragraph (should contain: who, what, when, where, why):
Remainder of body text – Should include any relevant information to your products or services. Include benefits, why your product or service is unique. Also include quotes from staff members, industry experts or satisfied customers.
If there is more than 1 page use:
                    -more-

(The top of the next page):
Abbreviated headline (page 2)

Remainder of text:
(Restate Contact information after your last paragraph):
For additional information or a sample copy, Contact: (all Contact information)
Summarize product or service specifications one last time
Company History (try to do this in one short paragraph)
                    # # #
        (Indicates Press Release is finished)

---

*"I think there is something, more important
than believing: ACTION!!
The world is full of dreamers, there aren't enough who will move
ahead and begin to take concrete steps to actualize their vision."*

APPLYING THE PLAN

<u>Here's how it works:</u>

By now, I guess you're saying, "Carole have you flipped? I've spent *way* over five minutes learning this plan and I just can't see how it would take me only five minutes to implement. Why do you call it **The Five-Minute Business Plan**?

Well guys it's like almost anything else you learn. It might take a long time to learn it, but not a long time to implement it. For instance, it might take you all day to learn to ride a bike - or like me forever - but once you've mastered the basics, it only takes a few minutes to ride that bike from one corner to the next.

The Five-Minute Business Plan's objective is to help you master the fundamentals so that you can run it in your head – I've done it hundreds of times – or on paper to see if your dream or idea is worth following up. If you've deemed your dream is worth pursuing, use the basics of **The Five-Minute Business Plan** to map out the particulars. When you've done that you can then turn your basic mapped out plan, if you want, into a standardized business plan. Most importantly, it takes the fear out of creating the big scary business plan.

Never again be afraid to dream, never again be afraid to turn that dream into a concrete plan.

If you have mastered the basics, you should be able to, in five minutes, evaluate your plan. You need satisfactory answers to the basics in order to proceed with your business idea.

THE BASICS

YOUR /MISSION/ *VISION* STATEMENT

YOU WANT TO KNOW:
How does your company change the world?

YOUR *PRODUCT/*SERVICE

YOU WANT TO KNOW:
How many other products like yours are out there.   What's your Competitive Edge?

YOUR *PLACE (S)* OF OPERATION

YOU WANT TO KNOW:
Can you make your business accessible to your Target Market?

YOUR *PRICING.* START UP COST/FIXED COSTS

YOU WANT TO KNOW:
Can I put together the money to start? Can I Make a Profit?

YOUR PROMOTION

YOU WANT TO KNOW
What is the Best Way to Tell My Target Market About My Business?

You are now on your way to your dream.
Happy planning!

Useful Business Reports:

- 90-Day Start Up Cost Worksheet

- 101 Ways for Your Business to Change the World

- Should I Incorporate My Business

- A Little Known Secret to Raising Capital for your Business

- Establishing Business Credit

- Selecting the Right Business Name

- The Benefit of Trademarking – What is a Trademark?

- Free Press Release Sites

You can find these and other business reports at
www.justwhatineeded2.com.
Some are free others no more than $2.00.

**Please contact Times Training Group for
The Five-Minute Business Plan
Workshop**

**TIMES TRAINING GROUP
carole @ bizmoneygo.com
www.Justwhatineeded2.com
888 272 7092**

I dream for love
With crazy things
Butterflies talking
Men with wings
Silver sidewalks, golden streets
Bumble bees singing
The latest beat
I dream...

I dream for love
With crazy things
Transparent bodies
Only hearts are seen
Yes! There is
A cosmic love that would not die
Souls touching the sky
I dream...
For you and I

DREAM TO BE SEEN
Jerald Times